sew a
Modern
Halloween

make 15 spooky projects for your home

Riel Nason

C&T PUBLISHING

DEDICATION

For Eli and Tess,
my favorite people to sew things for

ACKNOWLEDGMENTS

Thank you to my agent, HILARY MCMAHON.

Thank you to KARLA MENAUGH for her fabulous job as my editor.

To TIMELESS TREASURES FABRICS AND RILEY BLAKE DESIGNS, thank you for providing me with fabric to use for some of the projects in this book. I am so pleased with the wonderful modern Halloween and basic fabrics I was sent by both companies, and I think they add so much style to the completed pieces.

Thank you to the WRITING AND ARTS COMMUNITIES for being supportive and encouraging of what I do.

Thank you to EVERYONE WHO LET ME KNOW THEY ENJOYED MY FIRST QUILT BOOK, *Modern Selvage Quilting* (from C&T Publishing), and suggested that I write another.

Thanks to SHANE, ELI, AND TESS for tolerating the sound of my sewing machine running in the background of their lives.

Text copyright © 2017 by Riel Nason

Photography and artwork copyright © 2017 by C&T Publishing, Inc.

PUBLISHER: Amy Marson

CREATIVE DIRECTOR: Gailen Runge

EDITOR: Karla Menaugh

TECHNICAL EDITOR: Helen Frost

COVER DESIGNER: Christina Jarumay Fox

BOOK DESIGNER: April Mostek

PRODUCTION COORDINATOR: Tim Manibusan

PRODUCTION EDITOR: Alice Mace Nakanishi

ILLUSTRATOR: Mary E. Flynn

PHOTO ASSISTANTS: Carly Jean Marin and Mai Yong Vang

HAND MODEL: Kristi Visser

COVER AND STYLE PHOTOGRAPHY by Lucy Glover and **INSTRUCTIONAL PHOTOGRAPHY** by Diane Pedersen of C&T Publishing, Inc., unless otherwise noted

Published by C&T Publishing, Inc., P.O. Box 1456, Lafayette, CA 94549

Attention Teachers: C&T Publishing, Inc., encourages you to use this book as a text for teaching. Contact us at 800-284-1114 or ctpub.com for lesson plans and information about the C&T Creative Troupe.

We take great care to ensure that the information included in our products is accurate and presented in good faith, but no warranty is provided, nor are results guaranteed. Having no control over the choices of materials or procedures used, neither the author nor C&T Publishing, Inc., shall have any liability to any person or entity with respect to any loss or damage caused directly or indirectly by the information contained in this book. For your convenience, we post an up-to-date listing of corrections on our website (ctpub.com). If a correction is not already noted, please contact our customer service department at ctinfo@ctpub.com or at P.O. Box 1456, Lafayette, CA 94549.

Trademark (™) and registered trademark (®) names are used throughout this book. Rather than use the symbols with every occurrence of a trademark or registered trademark name, we are using the names only in the editorial fashion and to the benefit of the owner, with no intention of infringement.

Printed in China

10 9 8 7 6 5 4 3 2 1

contents

-- **PROJECTS** --

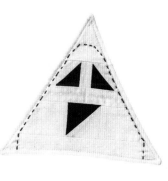

introduction

I'm pretty sure some of the most difficult decisions of my childhood involved what to wear for Halloween.

Successful costume choices included the Queen of Hearts, an elephant, a mummy—and once, even a superhero! Or kind of. My mother made my shorts, shirt, cape, and hat from a gold patterned upholstery fabric. Blue felt trim was added, and red tights finished the outfit. I looked fabulous (or thought I did, anyway).

But oh, how hard it was every year to narrow all the possibilities down to just one. I had seemingly endless ideas. What figured into my decision-making process was not only what would be fun to wear, but what would be fun to make—to create. When I was young, my crafty mother brought my ideas to fruition and never disappointed me. As I got older, it was I who, even though I didn't sew much, continued to gather, construct, draw, paint, glue, and otherwise assemble my costumes.

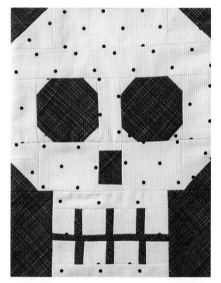

Now that I have children of my own, the innovation and improvisation haven't stopped. They come up with the ideas, and I, often with their help, make the costumes. For example, when my son was four, he sure made a cute lighthouse.

Creativity will always be a huge part of Halloween, and that is one of the main reasons I love it. No matter how many decorations manufacturers continue to mass produce and sell in stores, the one very best Halloween display item is something that you use your own creativity for. Know what I'm talking about? A jack-o'-lantern. How do you turn a plain old pumpkin into something magical? You carve it yourself. You decide how it will look. You cut out the design. You perform the makeover, and complete the transformation. It is the original seasonal DIY project.

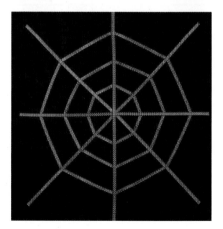

But Halloween projects you've made yourself don't have to stop at the porch. Or they don't have to be costumes you wear. We quilters can do much more than that. If you're reading this book, I'd bet you want to do much more than that.

It's time to express your Halloween creativity in fabric. It's time to make pillows and quilts and table runners to place throughout your home. Like the projects on these pages. So let's get started.

modern halloween sewing

Making It Spooky, Yet Stylish

Halloween isn't meant to be cute. Leave that for the Easter Bunny. Or at least Halloween for adults doesn't have to be cute. There will be no smiling bats wearing pink hair bows here. Halloween is the one time of year to embrace the spookier, scarier side of things. The designs in this book are for the modern and mature Halloween enthusiast (doesn't that sound official?). Really, these are projects that can add a unique seasonal touch to your home without making it seem like you have decorated the place for a preschool party.

The designs are purposefully modern. They use simple angular shapes and feature areas of negative space (or space filled with a single fabulous, carefully chosen Halloween fabric). Some designs are quite subtle, with minimal details. Sometimes solid fabrics are used along with Halloween prints and modern basics. The projects here aim to be slightly scary but chic.

Choosing Colors and Fabrics

Modern Halloween fabrics (Many of these fabrics are from the Wicked / Wicked Eve collection, by Timeless Treasures Fabrics.)

Modern basic fabrics (Several of these fabrics are from Riley Blake Designs and Timeless Treasures Fabrics.)

Fabrics that have a mature, subtly spooky appearance complete the look of the modern designs. The color scheme is essential as well. Orange and black are go-to colors for Halloween, but these colors are then complemented by shades of cream, ivory, gray, and charcoal. Purple and lime green, which often show up in Halloween fabrics targeted to a younger audience, are left out completely.

Not every fabric in your project needs to have black cats or ghosts on it. Less is often more. Combining Halloween-themed fabrics with modern basics will make the overall look more stylish and contemporary. So what are possibilities for basics? Be bold. Don't reach only for safe tone-on-tone blenders. Try for geometrics—dots, herringbones, or hexagons.

Use crosshatches, chevrons, tossed triangles or rectangles, tiny lines, or stripes. Consider large-scale patterns that look as though they could be wallpaper in a haunted house. Think about designs that aren't necessarily sold as Halloween fabrics but would work. Some possibilities are wood grain (haunted house), twigs and branches and leaves (spooky woods), dark clouds, a night sky, or bugs.

Check your stash. You may already have some fabrics you can use. Even if you are purchasing new fabric, resist the urge to buy 100 percent Halloween designs. Your projects will have a more distinctive look if you mix in some basics and unique choices. Also, try to buy fabrics from several different Halloween lines and manufacturers. Challenge yourself to mix and match.

About the Designs and Projects

Everyone crafts at a different pace, but none of these projects should involve a huge investment of time. I can understand not wanting to spend months creating an heirloom-quality Halloween piece that will be displayed for only a few weeks a year. Some projects can be made in a couple of hours or in an afternoon; some can easily be made in a weekend. In any event, you certainly don't have to start working on these Halloween projects in July to be sure they are done in time (that is, unless you want to).

Each section opener includes a basic technique or block pattern and then specific projects with complete, detailed instructions. The designs involve straight-ahead basic piecing and no paper piecing, as well as several chances for improvisational cutting and sewing. You will have many opportunities to truly express your own creativity in what you make.

Beyond the Designs and Projects

Because these projects include instructions for a basic design or block as a starting point, if you're so inclined or inspired, you can then do your own thing completely from there.

Maybe you like a block that I suggest turning into a table runner but think it would look cool as a whole quilt. Or perhaps as an accent pillow. Sounds great, do it. Maybe you see a design technique that inspires you to make something entirely different than anything shown here. Again, do it. All the projects made just the way the instructions are written will give you fabulous results, but there is always the possibility for so much more. I love to look at these designs and think about how they evolved. So feel free to embrace the creativity of Halloween and see what happens when you start your own seasonal sewing.

Scrappy Jack

Projects made with Basic Scrappy Jack block (page 8)

It seems only right to start the book with projects made featuring the most traditional of Halloween decorations—the jack-o'-lantern. And just as you improvise when you carve a real pumpkin, you can do much the same with fabric in these projects. Piece the jack-o'-lantern with scraps following this method to create your own look.

basic scrappy jack block

FINISHED BLOCK: 12″ × 12″

Instructions are for making a single Scrappy Jack block.

MATERIALS

Black fabric:

• 3 pieces no smaller than 3″ × 3″

• 1 scrap no smaller than 3″ × 6″

Orange fabric: Many scraps of all sizes

CUTTING

This is an improvisational technique/block, so cutting is not done with exact measurements. The estimates given are to keep the proportional size of eyes-to-nose-to-mouth the same as in the completed blocks shown here.

> **tip** This block is very much make-it-up-as-you-go-along. I know not everyone is comfortable with this, so you might want to cut out a paper square 12½″ × 12½″ (the trim size of the block you are making) like a little design wall / test block to place the pieces on as you go. Then you can see if you like the size and spacing of the eyes, nose, and mouth before sewing everything together. A test block will also let you see how many scraps you need to make the block big enough—keeping in mind that the ¼″ seam allowance will make everything a little smaller when sewn.

Eyes

• Use 2 of the 3″ black squares to cut the eye shapes, which are triangles with all 3 sides approximately the same length. Each side should be about 2½″– 3½″ long.

Nose

• Use 1 of the 3″ black squares to cut the nose shape. The nose shape is a longer triangle with a smaller base and longer sides. The base should be about 1½″ across and the height should be about 2″–2½″.

Mouth

• Use the 3″ × 6″ black rectangle to make the mouth. The mouth should be an elongated triangle with 1 short side about 2″–3″ long and the 2 other sides each about 6″ long.

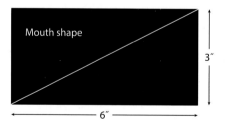

An easy way to cut mouth shape is to cut rectangle diagonally.

Orange Scraps

• Prepare the scraps by cutting several strips between 2″ and 2½″ wide and at least 4″–5″ in length (longer is better). The pieces do not have to be of uniform width.

• Cut the rest of the pieces to size during construction.

Construction

Use a ¼″ seam allowance and press the seams open.

MAKE THE EYES

1. Add a complete scrap border around each eye. Select a scrap strip slightly longer than the first side of the first triangle. Sew. Press. Trim the excess so that the strip edge is continuous with the side of the triangle.

Repeat with the second strip. This time you only need to trim the edge of the strip on the side where the third strip will be placed. Sew the third strip in place. Do not trim. Press.

Repeat the process for the second eye.

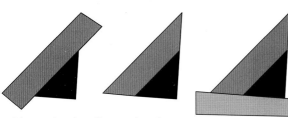

Add scrap border all around each eye.

2. Place the eyes side by side. The eyes shown in the diagram have the sides without the scraps trimmed in the middle next to each other, but you can rotate the eyes any way you wish. You decide what looks best. Sew the eye sections together in the center. You may wish to sew them perfectly straight, or you may wish to sew at a slight angle. You may also overlap pieces by much more than the ¼″ seam allowance in order to position them the way you like. Just trim the seam allowance to ¼″ after sewing. Press.

3. Add more scrap strips to the outer edges of the eyes. You can add pieces perfectly straight or at an angle. Add pieces until the eye section is at least 12½″ wide at the point where you estimate you might trim it. Press.

> **tip** For an even scrappier look, you can always sew two scraps together first to make a single larger one before using it in the block.

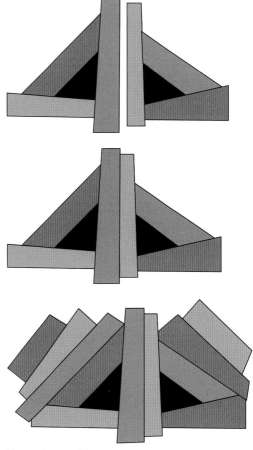

Eye unit assembly

MAKE THE NOSE

1. Select 2 scrap strips just slightly wider than the nose piece. Place the nose at one end of each strip and cut the strip at the same angle as the nose, as if you are using the side of the nose as a template.

2. Sew the scrap strips to each side of the nose. Press. Trim the bottom of the nose even with the bottom of the strips.

3. Add additional scrap strips to each end of the pieced strip to make the entire width about 12½″, with the nose in the center.

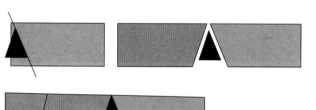

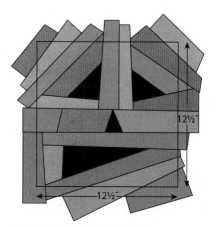

Nose unit assembly

MAKE THE MOUTH

Following the same instructions as for placing a scrap border around an individual eye (page 9), add a border around the mouth. Add a few additional strips on the bottom and sides to make the width about 12½″.

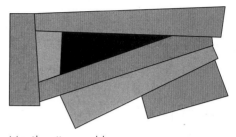

Mouth unit assembly

ASSEMBLE THE BLOCK

1. Following the face assembly diagram, sew the three rows of eye unit, nose unit, and mouth unit together. Press.

2. At this point, if the block is larger than 12½″ × 12½″, you may move on to trimming the block. If the block is too small, or you just feel like improvising a bit more, add additional strips. You may wish to slice corners or sections off a bit to add new scraps. You may wish to add 1 long strip on any of the sides to easily make the block bigger. Do whatever. This is part of the fun of improvising!

3. Trim the block to 12½″ × 12½″. Be careful to center the face when you do this.

4. Staystitch ⅛″–¼″ from the outer edge of the block so that none of the seams pull loose.

And there you go! Scrappy pumpkin perfection! (Say that ten times fast.)

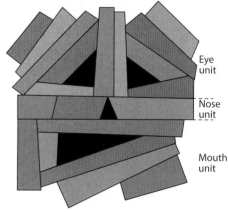

Face assembly

Eye unit

Nose unit

Mouth unit

Trim block to 12½″ × 12½″.

12½″

12½″

scrappy jack bits and pieces quilt

Designed and made by Riel Nason, quilted by Tina Hanson
FINISHED BLOCK: 12″ × 12″
FINISHED QUILT: 60″ × 72″

MATERIALS

Yardages are based on fabric that is at least 40″ wide.

Background fabric: 4 yards for blocks

Black scraps: Enough for 1 Scrappy Jack block (page 8)

Orange scraps: Many for Scrappy Jack block and scrappy trim on background blocks

Orange Halloween fabric (optional or additional): ¼ yard each of 4–8 different orange Halloween fabrics, if you don't have a really large scrap pile or if you plan to make a scrappy binding as well

Binding: ⅝ yard, or use orange scraps to make a scrappy binding

Backing: 4 yards (pieced crosswise)

Batting: 64″ × 76″

CUTTING

Background fabric

• Cut 10 strips 12½″ × width of fabric.

  Subcut 29 squares 12½″ × 12½″.

Scrappy Jack block and scrappy triangles

• Cut pieces for Scrappy Jack block and scrappy triangles on blocks during construction.

Binding

• Cut 8 strips 2½″ × width of fabric, or cut equivalent in scraps for a scrappy binding.

Construction

Use a ¼" seam allowance and press the seams open.

MAKE THE BLOCKS

1. Refer to Basic Scrappy Jack Block (page 8) to make 1 Scrappy Jack block.

2. Sew an orange fabric scrap at an angle across either 1 or 2 corners of a 12½" background square. Check that the scrap is large enough to cover the area. Then flip the scrap away from the corner so that the scrap and the background square are right sides together. Sew along the edge of the scrap. Flip the scrap back to its proper position. Press. Use the edge of the background square as a guide to trim the corner. Then cut away the background fabric underneath, leaving a ¼" seam allowance. Press again.

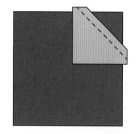

> **tip** As mentioned in the instructions for making the Scrappy Jack Block, to make the blocks even scrappier, you can sew 2 scraps together here before sewing them at an angle across the corners of the background squares. This gives even more interest and variety to the quilt—as well as allowing you to use up small pieces.

3. Sew as many orange-scrap triangles on as many blocks as you wish. You can sew a scrap on every square or leave some without any. (In my quilt there are 4 plain squares.) But this is *your* quilt, so do whatever you think looks best.

MAKE THE QUILT TOP

1. Arrange the blocks according to the quilt assembly diagram. The Scrappy Jack block is in the fourth position in the second row. Place scrappy and plain background blocks however you like.

2. Sew 6 rows of 5 blocks each. Press.

3. Sew the rows together to complete the quilt top. Press.

Quilt assembly

FINISH THE QUILT

Quilt and bind as desired.

> **tip** It is completely up to you what you choose as binding, but I highly recommend a scrappy binding made with the same orange fabrics as in the quilt blocks. Even if you use a plain fabric binding, perhaps mix in a few scrappy pieces here and there to reflect the random scrappiness of the quilt blocks.

Cuddle up with your new friend, Scrappy Jack!

big scrappy jack pillow

Designed and made by Riel Nason

FINISHED BLOCK: 12″ × 12″

FINISHED PILLOW: 20″ × 20″

MATERIALS

Yardages are based on fabric that is at least 40″ wide.

Background fabric: 1 yard for pillow front border and backing

Black scraps: Enough for 1 Scrappy Jack block (page 8)

Orange scraps: Many for Scrappy Jack block and pillow corners

Lining: 23″ × 23″ (will be inside the pillow and will not show, so it can be an ugly fabric you want to use up)

Batting: 23″ × 23″

Perle cotton: Orange or variegated red/orange for accent quilting

Pillow form: 20″ × 20″

CUTTING

Background fabric

• Cut 2 strips 4½″ × width of fabric.

  Subcut 2 rectangles 4½″ × 20½″ and 2 rectangles 4½″ × 12½″ for pillow front border.

• Cut 1 strip 20½″ × width of fabric.

  Subcut 2 rectangles 15″ × 20½″ for pillow backing.

Scrappy Jack block and scrappy triangles

• Cut pieces for Scrappy Jack block and scrappy triangles at pillow corners during construction.

Construction

Use a ¼″ seam allowance and press the seams open.

MAKE THE PILLOW FRONT

1. Refer to Basic Scrappy Jack Block (page 8) to make 1 Scrappy Jack block.

2. Sew a 4½″ × 12½″ border to the sides of the Scrappy Jack block. Press.

3. Sew a 4½″ × 20½″ border to the top and bottom of the Scrappy Jack block. Press.

4. Add a triangle to each corner of the pillow, using the same method as described for adding scrappy triangles to the corners of the blocks in the *Scrappy Jack Bits and Pieces Quilt* (see Make the Blocks, page 12). Press.

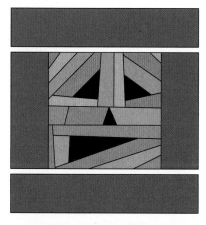

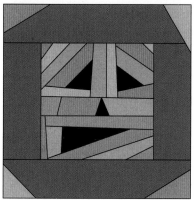

Pillow front assembly

5. Layer the lining, batting, and pillow front. Quilt as desired. For an additional accent, add hand-sewn stitches in perle cotton along a few (or all) of the quilted lines. Trim to 20½" × 20½".

MAKE THE ENVELOPE BACK

1. On a 20½" edge of 1 of the backing rectangles, turn and press a ¼" fold and then a ½" fold. This encloses the raw edge of the fabric. Sew. Press.

2. Using the other backing rectangle, repeat Step 1, but make the second fold 1".

- -

MAKE THE PILLOW

1. Place the pillow front on a flat surface with its right side facing up. Place the pillow backing rectangle with the 1" hem right side down over the front, with the sewn edge toward the center. Align the raw edges of the rectangle with the bottom of the pillow front.

2. Place the other backing rectangle so that its right side also faces toward the pillow front. Align the raw edges of the rectangle with the top of the pillow, with the sewn edge toward the center. The 2 rectangles will overlap in the middle.

3. Pin and sew the outer edge. Backstitch several times where the edges of the backing rectangles overlap to give this area added strength.

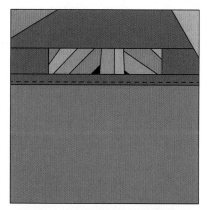

Pillow assembly

- -

FINISH THE PILLOW

1. Turn right side out. Make sure the corners are completely pushed out.

2. Place the pillow form inside.

Toss this pumpkin pillow proudly onto your couch.

scrappy jack halloween treat pillow

Designed and made by Riel Nason

FINISHED PILLOW: Approximately 6″ × 24″

MATERIALS

Yardages are based on fabrics at least 40″ wide.

Orange Halloween fabric: Many scraps

Halloween fabric A: ¼ yard for pillow borders

Halloween fabric B: ¼ yard for pillow borders

Halloween fabric C: 1 yard for pillow cuffs

Ribbon: 1 yard for pillow ties

Pillow form: 6″ × 14″ neck roll

CUTTING

Halloween fabric A

- Cut 2 strips 2½″ × width of fabric.

  Subcut 2 strips 2½″ × 21″.

Halloween fabric B

- Cut 2 strips 2″ × width of fabric.

  Subcut 2 strips 2″ × 21″.

Halloween fabric C

- Cut 2 strips 16″ × width of fabric.

  Subcut 2 rectangles 16″ × 21″.

Scrappy Jack block

- Cut scraps during construction.

Ribbon

- Cut 2 lengths 18″.

Construction

Use a ¼″ seam allowance and press the seams open.

MAKE THE PILLOW CENTER

1. For this project make a faceless variation of the Scrappy Jack block and trim it to 7″ × 21″. Follow the improvisational techniques discussed in Basic Scrappy Jack Block (page 8).

If you are unsure of how to start, a good way is to pretend you are making 2 eyes from the instructions, but use an orange scrap in the middle instead of a black one. Build up the scraps around these eye bits and then eventually sew them together. Turn the unit sideways. Add more scraps as needed to elongate the piece. Or start as if making a single eye and build from there, adding pieces at an angle.

2. When the piece is large enough, trim it to 7″ × 21″ and staystitch ⅛″–¼″ from the outer edge of the block.

3. Sew a 2½″ × 21″ strip of Halloween fabric A to each side of the scrappy pieced unit. Press.

4. Sew a 2″ × 21″ strip of Halloween fabric B to each side. Press.

Pillow center assembly

ADD THE PILLOW CUFFS

1. Referring to the pillow cuff assembly diagram, add a cuff to one end of the pieced center. Place a 16″ × 21″ fabric C cuff rectangle right side up on a flat surface, with a long edge at the top. Place the pieced center on top, right side down and with long edges aligned. Slightly roll up the pieced center toward the aligned edges, exposing the cuff fabric beneath.

2. Lift the bottom edge of the cuff fabric up and over the pieced center. Align the long edge of the cuff fabric with the 2 layers at the top edge. Pin the top edge. There should be 3 layers—the fabric, the pieced center, and the other edge of the fabric. Sew the top edge with a ¼″ seam, backstitching at the start and finish.

3. Turn right side out. Press. The pieced center will now have a cuff of the fabric with no raw edges showing on either side.

4. Using the remaining 16″ × 21″ cuff rectangle, repeat Steps 1–3 on the other end of the pieced center. Press.

FINISH THE PILLOW

1. To sew the pillow cover together with an enclosed seam, fold the pillow cover in half lengthwise with the *wrong* sides together, matching the seams at the fabric cuffs. Pin. Sew the long edge with a ¼″ seam. Press.

2. Trim the seam allowance to ⅛″.

3. Turn the pillow with *right* sides together. Sew the same edge with a ¼″ seam. Turn right side out.

4. Pull the pillow cover over the pillow form. Center the cover so that the ends of the pillow form align with the ends of the center section, with the fabric cuffs extending beyond.

5. Using a ribbon piece for each end, gather the fabric that extends beyond the form and tie it closed. Use a double knot, making it nice and tight. Then tie in a bow.

All done! And see, it really wasn't tricky to make this treat!

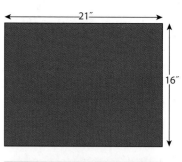

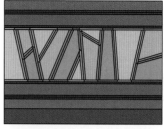

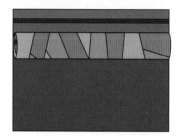

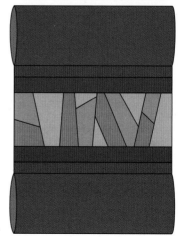

Pillow cuff assembly

Bone Appétit

Projects made with Basic Skull block (page 18)

Stylish skulls definitely fit in with the scary chic feel of the projects here. Simple bold skulls made in just two fabrics work perfectly with busier Halloween prints in large blocks.

basic skull block

FINISHED BLOCK: 6¾" × 8¾"

FINISHED BLOCK WITH BORDERS: 9¾" × 11¾"

Instructions are for making a single skull block.

MATERIALS

Yardages are based on fabric at least 40" wide.

Skull fabric: ¼ yard

Background fabric: ¼ yard

Marking pen

CUTTING

To keep everything easy and organized, cutting and construction instructions are organized by section.

Forehead

Background fabric

• Cut 1 square 2½" × 2½".

Skull fabric

• Cut 1 square 2½" × 2½".

• Cut 1 rectangle 2" × 4¼".

• Cut 1 rectangle 1½" × 7¼".

Eyes

Background fabric

• Cut 2 squares 2½" × 2½".

Skull fabric

• Cut 8 squares 1" × 1".

• Cut 1 rectangle 1¼" × 2½".

• Cut 2 rectangles 1½" × 2½".

Nose

Background fabric

• Cut 1 square 2" × 2".

• Cut 1 rectangle 1¼" × 1½".

Skull fabric

• Cut 1 square 2" × 2".

• Cut 2 rectangles ¾" × 1¼".

• Cut 2 rectangles 1" × 1½".

• Cut 2 rectangles 2" × 2½".

Mouth

Background fabric

• Cut 3 rectangles ¾" × 2½".

• Cut 1 rectangle ¾" × 4¼".

• Cut 2 rectangles 2" × 3¼".

Skull fabric

• Cut 4 rectangles 1¼" × 2½".

• Cut 2 rectangles 1" × 4¼".

Borders

Background fabric

• Cut 2 rectangles 2" × 9¼".

• Cut 2 rectangles 2" × 10¼".

Construction

Use a ¼" seam allowance and press the seams open.

> **tip** These are small pieces, so please double-check the accuracy of your ¼" seam allowance so that everything matches nicely. But don't worry if everything doesn't look perfect. It is very tricky with pieces this small. Press carefully so the pieces don't distort in shape. Finally, use a short stitch length to prevent seam ends from opening.

FOREHEAD

1. Use the 2½" background fabric square and the 2½" skull fabric square to make 2 half-square triangle blocks. Place the squares right sides together. On the back of the skull fabric square, draw a diagonal line corner to corner.

2. Sew ¼" away from each side of the drawn line. Cut on the drawn line.

3. Press each unit open. Trim each to 2" × 2".

Make half-square triangle blocks.

4. Following the assembly diagram, sew a half-square triangle block to the ends of the 2" × 4¼" skull fabric rectangle. Press. Sew the completed unit to the top of the 1½" × 7¼" skull fabric rectangle. Press.

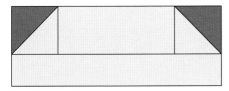

Forehead assembly

EYES

1. On the back of each 1" × 1" skull fabric square, draw a diagonal line corner to corner.

2. Place a square from Step 1 in each corner of the 2½" × 2½" background fabric squares, right sides together. Sew on each drawn line. Trim the seam allowance to ¼". Press.

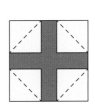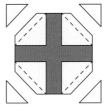

Make eyes.

3. Following the assembly diagram, sew a 1¼" × 2½" skull fabric rectangle between the 2 completed eye units. Add a 1½" × 2½" skull fabric rectangle to each end. Press.

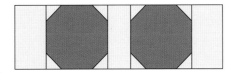

Eyes assembly

NOSE

1. Following the steps for making half-square triangles in the forehead instructions (at left), use the 2" × 2" background fabric square and the 2" × 2" skull fabric square to make 2 half-square triangles. Trim the blocks to 1½" × 1½".

2. Sew a 1" × 1½" skull fabric rectangle to the top of each half-square triangle to complete these units. Press.

3. Sew a ¾" × 1¼" skull fabric rectangle to the top and the bottom of the 1½" × 1¼" background fabric nose rectangle. Press.

4. Sew the 2" × 2½" skull fabric rectangles to the sides of the nose unit from Step 3. Add a pieced unit from Step 2 to each end to complete the nose unit.

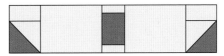

Nose assembly

MOUTH

1. Arrange and sew the 1¼" × 2½" skull fabric rectangles to the ¾" × 2½" background fabric rectangles, starting and ending with the skull fabric rectangles. Press.

2. Cut the sewn unit in half horizontally, making 2 rectangles 1¼" × 4¼".

3. Sew the ¾" × 4¼" background fabric rectangle between the 2 pieced rectangles. The finished unit will look like a row of teeth.

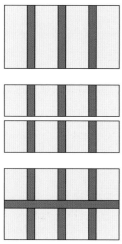

Teeth assembly

4. Sew a 1" × 4¼" skull fabric rectangle to the top and the bottom of the teeth unit to finish the mouth.

5. Following the mouth assembly diagram, sew 2" × 3¼" background fabric rectangles to the sides of the mouth unit.

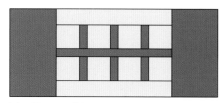

Mouth assembly

ASSEMBLE THE SKULL BLOCK

1. Following the skull block assembly diagram, sew the rows together. Press.

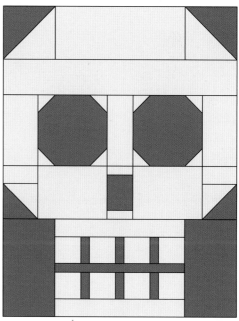

Skull block assembly

2. Sew 2" × 9¼" background fabric rectangles to the sides of the skull block as borders. Press.

3. Sew 2" × 10¼" background fabric rectangles to the top and bottom of the skull unit as borders to finish the block. Press.

Skull block with borders

All done ... and I'll bet it looks ex-skull-ent!

bone appétit
sideboard runner

Designed and made by Riel Nason

FINISHED BLOCK: 6¾" × 8¾"

FINISHED BLOCK WITH BORDERS: 9¾" × 11¾"

FINISHED RUNNER: 12¼" × 68¾"

MATERIALS

Yardages are based on fabric at least 40" wide.

Skull main fabric: ⅓ yard for skull blocks

Skull background fabric: ⅓ yard for skull blocks

Halloween fabric A: ⅓ yard for blocks

Halloween fabric B: ⅓ yard for blocks

Binding: ½ yard

Backing: 1 yard

Batting: 16" × 73"

CUTTING

Skull fabrics

- Referring to Basic Skull Block (page 18), follow the cutting and sewing instructions to make 2 skull blocks.

Halloween fabric A

- Cut 1 strip 10¼" × width of fabric.

  Subcut 3 rectangles 10¼" × 12¼".

Halloween fabric B

- Cut 1 strip 10¼" × width of fabric.

  Subcut 2 rectangles 10¼" × 12¼".

Binding

- Cut 5 strips 2¼" × width of fabric.

Construction

Use a ¼" seam allowance and press the seams open.

MAKE THE RUNNER

1. Refer to Basic Skull Block (page 18) to make 2 skull blocks with borders.

2. Using the 10¼" × 12¼" fabric A and B rectangles, sew a fabric B rectangle to each side of a fabric A rectangle. Sew a skull block to each end of this unit. Add a fabric A rectangle to each end to complete the runner top. Press.

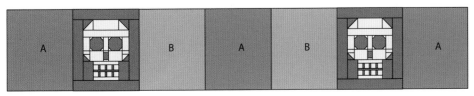

Runner assembly

FINISH THE RUNNER

Quilt and bind as desired.

Place on your sideboard under a spooky centerpiece.

bone appétit banner

Designed and made by Riel Nason

FINISHED BLOCK: 6¾" × 8¾"

FINISHED BANNER: 115" × 9"

MATERIALS

Yardages are based on fabric at least 40" wide.

Skull main fabric: ⅓ yard for skull blocks

Skull background fabric: ⅓ yard for skull blocks

Assorted Halloween fabrics (8): At least 7¼" × 9¼" each (could be large scraps or pieces cut from fat eighths or fat quarters)

White fabric: ¾ yard for backing rectangles

Halloween fabric: ¼ yard for banner string

CUTTING

Skull fabrics

• Referring to Basic Skull Block (page 18), follow the cutting and sewing instructions to make 3 skull blocks *without the border pieces.*

Assorted Halloween fabrics for blocks

• Cut 8 rectangles 7¼" × 9¼".

White fabric

• Cut 3 strips 7¼" × width of fabric.

  Subcut 11 rectangles 7¼" × 9¼".

Halloween fabric for banner string

• Cut 3 strips 2" × width of fabric.

  Trim strips to 2" × 40".

Construction

Use a ¼" seam allowance.

MAKE THE BANNER BLOCKS

1. Make 3 skull blocks (page 18). Since you are *not* adding the outer borders, the skull blocks should measure 7¼" × 9¼" including seam allowances.

2. Attach a backing rectangle to each of the 3 skull blocks and all 8 Halloween fabric rectangles. Place a Halloween fabric rectangle or skull block right sides together with a backing rectangle. Sew around 3 sides, leaving the top side unsewn. Turn inside out. Be sure the corners are poked all the way out. Press. Repeat for the remaining blocks and rectangles.

MAKE THE BANNER STRING

1. Sew the 3 banner strips together with diagonal seams, just as you would to make binding. (Overlap strip ends at 90°, sew across the overlapped area diagonally. Trim excess to ¼″ seam allowance.) Press.

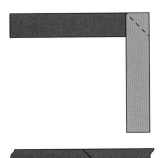

Sew strips together with diagonal seams.

2. Next, turn the strip into a string, much like a seam binding. Press the entire length of the strip in half lengthwise, wrong sides together.

3. Place the strip flat on the ironing board and open it so that the wrong side faces up. Fold each long raw edge in to meet the line that you just pressed. Press along the entire length.

4. Fold the strip again on the original pressed line. Press again.

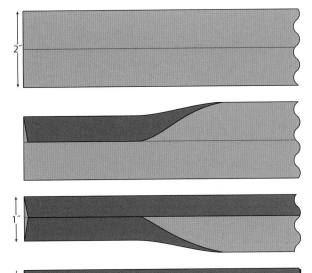

Make banner string.

5. Fold the strip in half lengthwise to find the center. Mark the center position with a pin.

MAKE THE BANNER

1. Arrange the blocks right side up according to the banner assembly diagram.

2. Position the center of the middle skull block in the very center of the banner string, using the pin as a guide. Continue placing blocks from the center outward. Leave a 2″ space between blocks.

3. Pin blocks in place as you go. Push the blocks between the folded layers of the string so that the top of the block touches the top inside the fold. This makes everything nice and secure.

4. At each end of the banner string, open the string and fold the raw edge under ½″. Refold to make a finished edge before you sew.

5. Sew the first finished end and then along the bottom edge of the banner string, securing the blocks in place. Finish by sewing the other end of the string closed.

Now there's nothing left to do except hang it up!

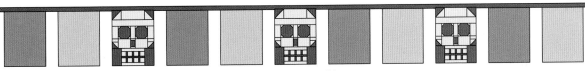

Banner assembly

On the Web

Projects made with Basic Spiderweb design (page 25)

Sew a Modern Halloween

A single spiderweb is the basic decoration on these pieces. Either selvages or ribbons can be used in a simple appliqué. Selvages are fun to incorporate, as they are white, just like a real web, but they also lure you in for a closer look with their unexpected bits of text. Choose selvages from Halloween fabrics and your wordy web may be filled with scary seasonal statements. Using ribbon allows you to choose any color—or even pattern, such as polka dots.

basic spiderweb design

Instructions are for making a single spiderweb.

MATERIALS

Background fabric: To fit the size of your project

Selvages or ribbon

Marking pen

Ruler with 45°-angle marking

Glue stick: For fabric use, nontoxic, washable

Thread: White (if using selvages) or colored (to match ribbon)

NOTE The length of ribbon and selvages needed for the projects will vary, depending on how you draw the web. The pattern estimates for the ribbon will be close to accurate, as ribbon can be cut continuously from a roll. For selvages, however, it is difficult to estimate because your selvage collection will likely consist of many pieces in various sizes. Before you start a project using selvages, look at what you have and do a trial-run layout to be sure you will have enough.

CUTTING

• Cut background fabric to size desired.

• Cut selvages or ribbon to size during construction.

Construction

MARK THE WEB

1. On the background fabric, find the spot that will be the center of the web. It does not have to be in the center of the fabric; choose wherever you'd like.

2. Using a marking pen, draw a vertical and a horizontal line through this point to make a large plus sign. You may extend the lines to the edges of the fabric if you would like the web to be that big, or make them shorter. Next, using the 45° angle on the ruler, draw 2 more lines intersecting the center point. This is the basic outline.

3. Begin to fill in the smaller internal web lines. Starting an absolute minimum of 1″ from the center point of the web, join each of the 8 long lines coming from the center with a short line in between.

NOTE For a large web, you may wish to start considerably further than 1″ from the center. Keep in mind the width of the selvages or ribbons that will eventually cover these marked lines. You do not want the design to look too crowded. You can choose to make the lines perfectly lined up with each other or slightly angled.

4. Repeat Step 3 twice to make 2 more rounds of internal lines, each spaced a minimum of 1″ apart (further apart for a larger web).

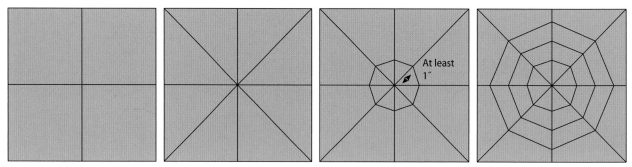

Mark web design.

Web Variations

The instructions above are to mark a full web. You may wish to mark a partial web, such as a half- or quarter web. To do this, place the center point in a corner or off to one side of the background. Measure as if making a full web, but mark only the lines you need on the background fabric.

You may also wish to make your web a bit different. There are several ways to do this.

• Try angling the main lines of the web at slightly more or less than 45° apart from each other.

• Add more lines between each of the main ones.

• Make inside lines significantly crooked.

• Leave a few of the internal lines out, as if there were a hole in the web.

• Randomly add a few extra internal lines.

Other possible designs are shown here (and I know you can think of more).

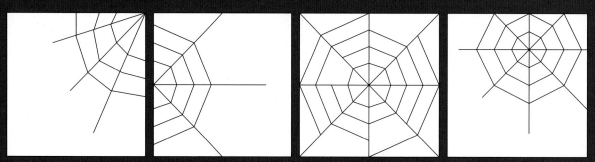

Alternate web designs

PREPARE THE SELVAGES

If you are using ribbon, skip this section.

1. Trim the selvages so just ¼" of fabric remains above the white part containing the text.

2. Fold and press this ¼" of fabric to the back of the selvage. (*Note: Be very careful not to burn or steam your fingers!*) From the front only the white of the selvage should now be visible.

ADD THE SELVAGES OR RIBBON

1. Place the selvage or ribbon pieces over all the small inner lines first, centering each piece above the drawn line. Cut each piece as you go, clipping at an angle on each end so that no pieces overlap. Do not worry about the raw unfinished edges. Later you will cover them with the longer selvages or ribbons.

2. Apply a small amount of glue on the back of each piece and smooth it into place. Let the glue dry.

3. Topstitch very close to the edge along each long side of every piece. By *very close* I mean only about ¹⁄₁₆" from the edge. On both the selvages and the ribbon, the sides are either finished or folded under so they will not pull loose after being topstitched down. Sew slowly so that you don't sew off the side of the selvage or ribbon. You may sew continuously around each complete circle of inner web lines. Do not worry about the raw edges at the end of each piece—you do not have to sew those down. Press.

4. Use 4 pieces of selvage or ribbon to cover the first 2 long web lines. It doesn't matter which set of 2 lines you do first, as long as you choose 2 that cross at a 90° angle. At the center, trim a small section out of each piece, leaving a little space so there is no overlap. These long web lines should cover and hide the raw edges of the inner web lines.

5. If your design has lines extending to the edges of the background, leave a raw edge at the end; later it will be sewn into a seam (or under the binding). If the lines do not extend all the way to the outside edge, fold under the end of each piece ¼"–½" to make a neat finished edge.

6. Apply glue to the back of each piece and smooth it into place. Let the glue dry. Topstitch along the long sides of each piece. Press.

7. Use 2 long selvage or ribbon pieces to cross over the center of the web and cover the remaining long lines. Apply glue and topstitch one in place. Press. Then apply glue and topstitch the other. Press. The pieces will overlap in the middle. Every raw edge on the web should now be covered.

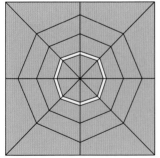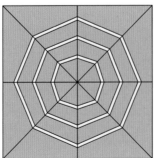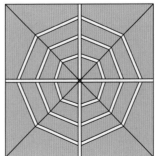

Assemble web.

Hope you are wowed by your wonderful web!

offset web mini quilt

Designed and made by Riel Nason
FINISHED QUILT: 18" × 24"

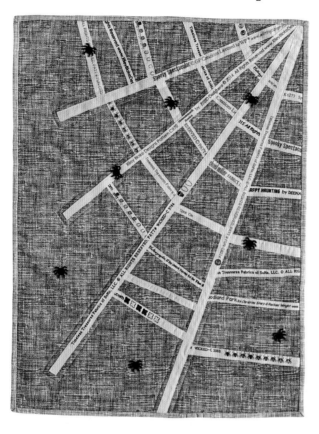

MATERIALS

Yardages are based on fabric that is at least 40" wide.

Background fabric: 5/8 yard

Selvages or ribbon: Approximately 5 yards

Marking pen

Glue stick: For fabric use, nontoxic, washable

Thread: White (if using selvages) or colored (to match ribbon)

Binding: 1/4 yard

Backing: 2/3 yard

Batting: 22" × 28"

Spider buttons: As embellishment (optional but recommended)

CUTTING

Background fabric

• Cut 1 strip 18" × width of fabric.

  Subcut 1 rectangle 18" × 24".

Selvages or ribbon

• Cut selvages or ribbon as you go during construction.

Binding

• Cut 3 strips 2¼" × width of fabric.

Construction

MAKE THE QUILT TOP

1. Referring to Web Variations (page 26), draw a web design radiating from the upper right corner of the background fabric.

2. Follow the construction steps in Basic Spiderweb Design (page 25) to sew selvages or ribbon to the web outline. Press.

FINISH THE QUILT

1. Quilt. Very simple quilting lines spaced just ¼" from the long vertical lines of the web are an easy possibility that looks good.

2. Bind the quilt.

3. If desired, add optional spider buttons as a finishing touch.

Done! Spiderrific!

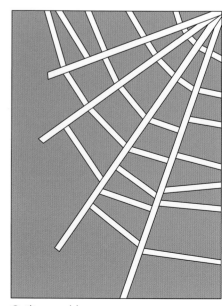

Quilt assembly

on the web pillow

Designed and made by Riel Nason

FINISHED PILLOW: 15" × 15"

MATERIALS

Yardages are based on fabric that is at least 40" wide.

Background fabric: ½ yard

Ribbon: Approximately 4 yards

Selvages (optional): 1 continuous piece at least 15½" long, as well as many other pieces

Glue stick: For fabric use, nontoxic, washable

Marking pen

Thread: White (if using selvages) or colored (to match ribbon)

Lining: 18" × 18" (This will be inside the pillow and will not show, so it can be an ugly fabric you want to use up.)

Batting: 18" × 18"

Pillow form: 16" × 16"

CUTTING

Background fabric

• Cut 1 strip 15½" × width of fabric.

Subcut 1 square 15½" × 15½" for pillow top.

Subcut 2 rectangles 12" × 15½" for pillow backing.

Selvages or ribbon

• Cut 1 length 15½".

• Cut other pieces to size as you go during construction.

Construction

Use a ¼" seam allowance and press the seams open.

DESIGN THE WEB

Referring to Basic Spiderweb Design (page 25), complete the web decoration on the 15½" × 15½" pillow front. You may wish to extend the web lines to the outside seams of the pillow, or you may prefer to make a smaller web centered in the top, as I did.

MAKE THE PILLOW FRONT

1. Layer the lining, batting, and pillow front. Quilt as desired. Press.

2. Trim excess backing and batting to 15½" × 15½".

NOTE You may find that the pillow front has shrunk a bit due to the application of the selvages (or ribbon) and quilting. If so, you may have to slightly trim the backing pieces of the pillow to match the size exactly.

MAKE THE ENVELOPE BACK

1. On a 15½" side of one of the backing rectangles, turn and press a ¼" fold and then a ½" fold. This encloses the raw edge of the fabric. Sew. Press.

2. Repeat Step 1, using the other backing rectangle, but make the second fold 1".

3. Glue a 15½" length of selvage or ribbon in place over the line you just stitched. Center the selvage or ribbon over the line so that the line is completely hidden. Topstitch on both long sides of the selvage or ribbon. Press.

MAKE THE PILLOW

1. Place the pillow front on a flat surface with its right side facing up. Place the backing rectangle with the selvage or ribbon applied to it right side down, with the sewn edge toward the center. Align the raw edges of the rectangle with the bottom of the pillow front.

2. Place the other backing rectangle so that its right side also faces toward the pillow front. Align the raw edges of the rectangle with the top of the pillow, with the sewn edge toward the center. The 2 rectangles will overlap in the middle.

3. Pin and sew all around the outer edge. Backstitch several times where the edges of the backing overlap to give this area added strength. It will be quite thick, especially where the selvage or ribbon trim is, so go slowly.

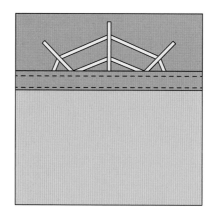

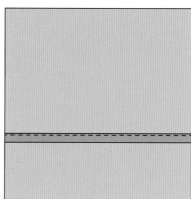

Pillow assembly

FINISH THE PILLOW

1. Turn the sewn pillow covering right side out. Make sure the corners are completely pushed out.

2. Place pillow form inside.

Toss the pillow onto that chair over there.

on the web curtain panel

Designed and made by Riel Nason

FINISHED PANEL: 26" × 52" *

*To fit a narrow, long window
(or adjust for your own window)*

> **NOTE** Windows obviously come in many different sizes, so if you'd like, please adjust length or width as necessary to fit yours. This project is designed so that the panel hangs flat and straight, without gathering, so the full design can be seen. Please take that into consideration if adjusting the project size.

MATERIALS

Yardages are based on fabric that is at least 40" wide.

Background fabric: 1²⁄₃ yards

Ribbon or selvages: 7–8 yards (estimated)

Marking pen

Glue stick: For fabric use, nontoxic, washable

Thread: White (if using selvages) or colored (to match ribbon)

CUTTING

Background fabric

• Cut 1 large rectangle 27½" × 57".

Selvages or ribbon

• Cut selvages or ribbon to size during construction.

Construction

MAKE THE CURTAIN PANEL

1. On a long side of the background rectangle, turn and press a ¼" fold and then a ½" fold. Topstitch the edge. Press. Repeat for the other side.

2. On the bottom of the background rectangle, turn and press a ½" fold and then a 1" fold. Topstitch the edge.

3. On the top of the background rectangle, turn and press a ½" fold and then a 3" fold. Topstitch the edge. Press.

4. To make the rod pocket, measure 1" down from the top of the curtain panel and sew a line parallel to the line that secured the edge.

APPLY THE WEB

1. Referring to Basic Spiderweb Design (page 25), design and apply the web. A large, bold web right in the center of the panel looks especially good.

2. Press.

Hang and enjoy!

Completed basic curtain panel

FRAMED FUSSY-CUT VARIATIONS

This is an easy variation of the spiderweb design method. But in this case, the selvages or ribbons will be used to make a frame around a fussy cut. The fussy cut doesn't need to be pieced in; the raw edges are held down and hidden by the frame in the same way that the raw edges of the web are hidden. So simple! These are fast and fun hostess gifts / party favors for your fellow adult Halloween lovers!

NOTE What is a fussy cut, you ask? It is a square or rectangle cut around a very specific part of a fabric design you choose to feature. It is often a single element of a design that you want to stand out.

basic framed fussy-cut design

Instructions are for making a single framed fussy cut.

MATERIALS

Scrap of fabric: With the design element you want to feature

Background fabric: To fit your project

Selvages or ribbon

Glue stick: For fabric use, nontoxic, washable

Thread: White (if using selvages) or colored (to match ribbon)

CUTTING

Fabric scrap

- Cut in the shape of a square or rectangle with chosen element in the center.

  It is best to limit either the length or the width to no more than 2½"–3" so that the piece will stay flat and secure when surrounded by the frame and not ripple in the middle when sewn to the finished piece. Also keep in mind that at least ¼" around the outside of the design will be overlapped by ribbon when it is framed, so be careful not to cut so close to the design element that part of it will end up being hidden.

Selvages or Ribbon

If using selvages, prepare them as if you were using them for a web design (page 27).

- Add 2"–3" to the length of the fussy cut (the size depends on how far you want the frame to extend). Cut 2 pieces to this length.

- Add 2"–3" to the width of the fussy cut. Cut 2 pieces to this length.

Construction

1. Using the glue stick, apply a thin line of glue on the back of the fussy-cut piece, around the outside edge.

2. Position the fussy-cut piece on the background fabric and smooth it into place.

3. For each ribbon or selvage piece that will be used as a vertical part of the frame, fold each short end under ¼" and press. Secure each end with a bit of glue if pressing doesn't make it stay folded.

4. Apply glue to the back of each ribbon or selvage piece and place one along each vertical side of the fussy-cut piece. Be sure that at least ¼" of the raw edge of the fussy-cut piece is under the ribbon or selvage. The ribbon or selvage piece extends beyond the fussy cut at both the top and bottom, so make sure the amount extending on each end is even. Let the glue dry.

5. Topstitch around the selvage piece or ribbon, about 1⁄16" from the edges. Press.

6. Repeat Steps 4 and 5 to apply the horizontal frame pieces. Press.

Fab-boo-lous!

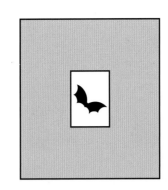

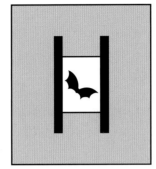

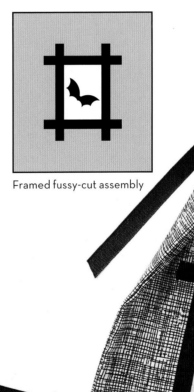

Framed fussy-cut assembly

Framed Fussy-Cut Gift Bag

Designed and made by Riel Nason
FINISHED BAG: 6" × 9"

MATERIALS

Yardages are based on fabric that is at least 40" wide.

Main fabric for bag: ¼ yard

Scrap of fabric: For fussy-cut piece

Ribbon: 18" for tie (selvages are not recommended for tie)

Ribbon or selvages: Lengths depend on size of fussy-cut piece (see Cutting, page 32).

Glue stick: For fabric use, nontoxic, washable

Thread: White (if using selvages) or colored (to match ribbon)

CUTTING

Main fabric for bag

• Cut 1 strip 7" × width of fabric.

   Subcut 2 rectangles 7" × 12".

Scrap for fussy cut

• Cut 1 rectangle or square. (Due to the small size of the bag, not larger than 2½" × 3" is best.)

Ribbon for tie

• Cut 1 length 18".

Ribbon or selvages for frame

• Cut lengths based on size of fussy-cut piece. See cutting directions for selvages or ribbon in Basic Framed Fussy-Cut Design (page 32).

Construction

Use a ¼" seam allowance.

1. On a short side of each 7" × 12" rectangle, turn and press a ½" fold and then a 2" fold. Topstitch ¼" from both the folded edge and the top of the rectangle. Press.

2. Following the instructions in Basic Framed Fussy-Cut Design (page 32), apply the fussy-cut piece to the lower middle section of the rectangle that will be the front of the bag. Be sure that the framed fussy cut is not so large that any of it will be lost in the seam allowance when the bag is sewn together.

3. Fold the ribbon tie in half to find the middle. On the right side of the back rectangle, center the ribbon 1" from the top. Sew a short line across the ribbon and backstitch several times to secure it in place.

NOTE These gift bags can easily be made a little larger if you wish. Just be sure to position the fussy cut accordingly.

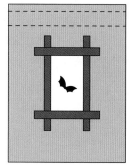

Front of bag before final assembly

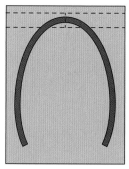

Back of bag before final assembly

4. Place the rectangles *wrong* sides together, matching the tops. Sew around 3 sides, leaving the folded edges at the top unsewn. Be careful not to accidentally sew over the tie; keep it tucked well out of the way.

5. Trim the ¼" seam to ⅛". Turn inside out so the *right* sides are together. Sew again around 3 sides with a ¼" seam. Again be careful not to sew over the tie.

6. Turn right side out. Press.

Remember, even if it turns out super-cute and you love it and want to keep it, you made it to give away. (Or keep the first one yourself and make another for a guest.)

Framed Fussy-Cut Wine Bag

Designed and made by Riel Nason

FINISHED BAG: 6" × 16" *

* To fit either a standard 750 mL or 1 L wine bottle

MATERIALS

Refer to the materials requirements for the Framed Fussy-Cut Gift Bag (previous page), *except* that you will need 24" of ribbon for the tie.

CUTTING

Main fabric for bag

• Cut 1 strip 7" × width of fabric.

  Subcut 2 rectangles 7" × 19".

Scrap for fussy cut

• Cut 1 rectangle or square. (Due to the size of the bag, not larger than 3" × 5" is best.)

Ribbon for tie

• Cut 1 length 24".

Ribbon or selvages for frame

• Cut lengths based on the size of the fussy-cut piece. See the cutting directions for selvages or ribbon in Basic Framed Fussy-Cut Design (page 32).

Construction

Use a ¼" seam allowance.

Using the 7" × 19" rectangles, follow the construction steps for the Framed Fussy-Cut Gift Bag (previous page). When you position the fussy-cut pieces, remember that the wine bottle will take up some space at the bottom of the bag, so place your design about halfway up the front.

*Admire your new bag.
I'm sure it looks wine-derful!*

Good? Night

Projects made with Basic Spooky Eyes design (page 37)

What is spookier than glowing eyes in the dark, indicating a creature you can't see the rest of? What if those eyes were peeking out from under your quilt? What if those eyes were *in* your quilt? See, I told you Halloween should be scary.

basic spooky eyes design

FINISHED BLOCK: 2¾" × 1¼"

Instructions are for making a single pair of eyes.

MATERIALS

Orange or yellow fabric: 1 square at least 2½" × 2½"

Black fabric: 1 square at least 5" × 5"

Marking pen

Ruler with a 45°-angle line

CUTTING

Orange or yellow fabric

• Cut 1 square 2½" × 2½".

 Subcut diagonally to make 2 triangles.

Black fabric

• Cut 1 square 2¼" × 2¼".

• Cut 1 rectangle ¾" × 3½".

• Cut 1 rectangle ¾" × 1¾".

Construction

Use a ¼" seam allowance and press the seams open.

> **tip** These eyes are very straightforward to make and give a great spooky result. But they are small pieces, so be careful with the accuracy of the ¼" seam. Also, press gently so you will not distort pieces. Use a short stitch length so seams do not come unsewn at the ends.

1. Sew the ¾" × 3½" black rectangle between the 2 long sides of the orange triangles. Press.

2. Trim the block to 2¼" × 2¼" square. Use the 45° line on the ruler to keep the black piece perfectly diagonal.

3. On the back of the pieced square, draw a line diagonally from corner to corner, perpendicular to the inserted black piece.

4. Place the pieced orange square and the 2¼" × 2¼" black square right sides together. Sew ¼" from each side of the drawn line. Cut on the drawn line. Press the triangles open to make the eye units. Trim the pieces to 1¾" × 1¾".

5. Sew the ¾" × 1¾" black rectangle between the 2 eye units as shown in the eye assembly diagram. Press.

Finished! Looking good!

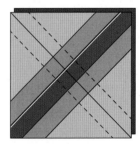

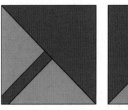

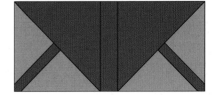

Eye assembly

good? night mini quilt

Designed and made by Riel Nason
FINISHED BLOCK: 2¾" × 1¼"
FINISHED QUILT: 15" × 19"

MATERIALS

Yardages are based on fabrics at least 40" wide.

Main fabric: ½ yard

Yellow or orange fabric: 1 square at least 2½" × 2½" for eyes

Black fabric: ¼ yard for eyes and eye background

Marking pen

Binding: ¼ yard

Backing: ½ yard

Batting: 19" × 23"

CUTTING

Eye fabrics

• Referring to Basic Spooky Eyes Design (page 37), follow the cutting and sewing instructions to make 1 block.

Main fabric

• Cut 1 rectangle 15" × 20".

Black fabric

• Cut 1 strip 5¼" × width of fabric.

  Subcut 1 rectangle 5¼" × 3½".

  Subcut 1 rectangle 5¼" × 9¼".

• Cut 1 rectangle 3¼" × 3".

• Cut 1 rectangle 3¼" × 1½".

Binding

• Cut 2 strips 2¼" × width of fabric.

Construction

Use a ¼" seam allowance and press the seams open.

MAKE THE EYES AND EYE BACKGROUND

1. Refer to Basic Spooky Eyes Design (page 37) to make 1 block.

2. Sew a 3¼" × 3" background rectangle to the top of the block. Press.

3. Sew a 3¼" × 1½" background rectangle to the bottom of the block. Press.

4. Sew a 5¼" × 3½" background rectangle to the right edge of the eye unit. Press.

5. Sew a 5¼" × 9¼" background rectangle to the left edge of the eye unit. Press.

Eye background assembly

QUILT ASSEMBLY

1. Cut a 3″ × 15″ piece from the bottom edge of the 15″ × 20″ main fabric rectangle. Set aside.

2. On the completed eye/background piece, measure and mark 2½″ from the bottom left corner. Using a long ruler, cut from this mark to the top right corner. Discard the top piece.

3. Align the bottom of the eye/background piece that you just trimmed with the bottom of the main fabric rectangle. Using the eye/background piece as a cutting guide, align a ruler along the top diagonal edge and cut the same angle across the background fabric. Discard the bottom piece of the main fabric.

4. Sew the top main fabric piece to the top of the eye/background piece.

5. Sew the 3″ × 15″ background rectangle from Step 1 to the bottom of the eye/background piece to complete the quilt top. Press.

FINISH THE MINI QUILT

Quilt and bind as desired.

Place on the wall to scare your visitors. Don't forget you put it there, though, and accidentally startle yourself on the way to the bathroom in the night.

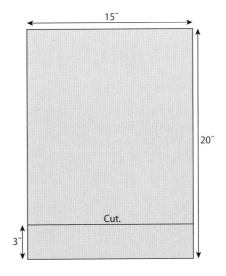

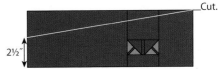

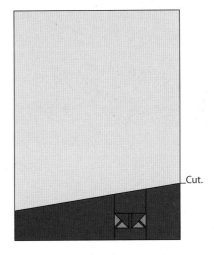

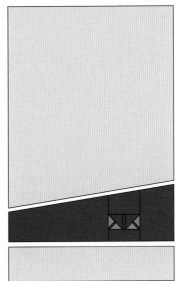

Quilt assembly

good? night lap quilt

Designed and made by Riel Nason, quilted by Tina Hanson

FINISHED BLOCK: 2¾" × 1¼"

FINISHED QUILT: 40" × 52"

tip This is a large project that goes together very quickly and lets the fabric do most of the work. Use this project as an opportunity to show off a larger-scale Halloween fabric that you just love.

MATERIALS

Main fabric: 1⅝ yards

Yellow or orange fabric: 3 squares each 2½" × 2½" for eyes

Black fabric: ½ yard for eyes and background

Marking pen

Binding: ½ yard

Backing: 2½ yards (pieced crosswise)

Batting: 44" × 56"

CUTTING

• Referring to Basic Spooky Eyes Design (page 37), follow the cutting and sewing instructions to make 3 blocks.

tip Three pairs of eyes are just the suggested minimum that makes this quilt super-quick to put together. Feel free to improvise and add in plenty more. If you do, just be careful with placement when piecing them into the black background so that you don't get so close to the quilt edges that they are lost in the seam allowance.

Main fabric

• Cut 1 rectangle 40" × 53".

Black fabric

• Cut 1 strip 3¼" × width of fabric.

 Subcut 2 rectangles 3¼" × 5".

 Subcut 1 rectangle 3¼" × 3¾".

 Subcut 1 rectangle 3¼" × 3½".

 Subcut 2 rectangles 3¼" × 2¼".

• Cut 1 strip 8" × width of fabric.

 Subcut 1 rectangle 8" × 17¼".

 Subcut 1 square 8" × 8".

 Subcut 1 rectangle 8" × 6".

 Subcut 1 rectangle 8" × 2".

Binding

• Cut 5 strips 2½" × width of fabric.

Construction

Use a ¼" seam allowance and press the seams open.

MAKE THE EYES AND EYE BACKGROUND

1. Refer to Basic Spooky Eyes Design (page 37) to make 3 blocks.

2. For the first block, sew a 3¼" × 5" black rectangle to the top and a 3¼" × 2¼" black rectangle to the bottom. Press.

3. For the second block, sew a 3¼" × 3¾" black rectangle to the top and a 3¼" × 3½" black rectangle to the bottom. Press.

4. For the third block, sew a 3¼" × 5" black rectangle to the top and a 3¼" × 2¼" black rectangle to the bottom. Press.

5. Sew together in this order, and then press:

A. 8" × 6" black rectangle	**D.** Second block
B. First block	**E.** 8" × 2" black rectangle
C. 8" × 17¼" black rectangle	**F.** Third block
	G. 8" × 8" black square

Eye/background assembly

QUILT ASSEMBLY

1. Cut an 8" × 40" rectangle from the bottom edge of the main background rectangle. Set aside.

2. On the completed eye/background piece, measure and mark 4" up from the bottom left corner. Use a long ruler or measuring tape to mark an angled line from this mark to the top right corner. Cut along the line. Discard the top piece.

> **tip** For a more detailed look at this process, see the construction diagrams for the *Good? Night Mini Quilt* (page 39).

3. Align the bottom of the eye/background piece that you just trimmed with the bottom of the main fabric rectangle. Using the eye/background piece as a cutting guide, align a ruler along the top diagonal edge and cut the same angle across the background fabric. Discard the bottom piece of the main fabric.

4. Sew the top main fabric piece to the top of the eye/background piece.

5. Sew the 8" × 40" main fabric rectangle from Step 1 to the bottom of the eye/background piece to complete the quilt top. Press.

Quilt assembly

FINISH THE QUILT

Quilt and bind as desired. A simple overall stipple or pantograph design would look good on this and not distract from the fun fabric you picked out.

Throw the quilt on the couch and try to nap without having nightmares.

Boo's Coming to Dinner?

Projects made with Basic Triangular Ghost block (page 43)

A ghost floats here and there on a table runner, place mat, and coaster set. Dress up your dining area with some spooky flair. These projects are a chance to mix and match many of your favorite Halloween and basic fabrics.

basic triangular ghost block

FINISHED BLOCK: 7⅝" per side
Instructions are for making a single ghost block.

MATERIALS

Yardages are based on fabrics at least 40" wide.

White fabric: ¼ yard

Black fabric: 1 piece at least 2" × 4"

60° triangle ruler: At least 8"

Marking pen

CUTTING

To keep everything easy and organized, cut pieces by section.

Forehead

White fabric

• Cut 1 rectangle 3¼" × 4".

Eyes

White fabric

• Cut 1 square 2" × 2".

• Cut 2 rectangles 1½" × 2".

• Cut 1 rectangle 1¼" × 6½".

• Cut 1 rectangle 1" × 1½".

Black fabric

• Cut 1 square 2" × 2".

Mouth

White fabric

• Cut 2 rectangles 2" × 3¼".

• Cut 1 square 2" × 2".

Black fabric

• Cut 1 square 2" × 2".

Neck

White fabric

• Cut 1 rectangle 1½" × 8½".

Construction

Use a ¼" seam allowance and press the seams open.

1. To make the half-square triangles for the eyes and mouth, mark a line diagonally from corner to corner on the back of the 2" × 2" white squares. Place each square right side together with a 2" × 2" black square.

2. For the eyes, stitch ¼" away from each side of the drawn line. Cut on the drawn line. Open and press. Trim each to 1½" × 1½" square.

3. For the mouth, stitch the squares together on the marked line. Trim the excess fabric on one side of the line, leaving a ¼" seam allowance. Open and press. It should be 2" square. Trim slightly if necessary to make it perfectly even.

Eyes assembly

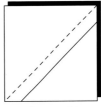

Mouth assembly

4. Sew the 1" × 1½" white rectangle between the eye half-square triangles. Sew the 1½" × 2" white rectangles to the sides of the eye half-square triangles. Press.

5. Sew the 2″ × 3¼″ white rectangles to the sides of the mouth half-square triangle. Press.

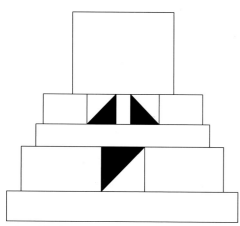

Ghost block assembly

6. Arrange the pieced eye and mouth rows with the remaining pieces. To ensure correct placement, align the rows at the centers. An easy way to do this is to fold each piece in half and lightly crease the center fold. Line up the center crease lines. Use pins to hold the perfect placement and to prevent the pieces from shifting while sewing.

7. Sew the rows together, using a small stitch length (you will be cutting through the seams and don't want the stitches to come loose). Press.

8. Trim the ghost block using a 60° triangle ruler. Line up the 7″ line on the bottom raw edge of the pieced ghost. The tip of the ruler will be about ½″ from the top edge. Hold securely and cut out the ghost block.

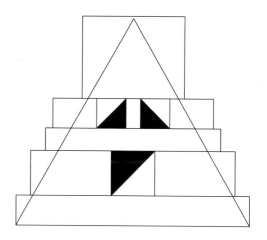

Finished—and that wasn't too scary a process, was it?

BOO'S COMING TO DINNER?
Complete Dining Set

Designed and made by Riel Nason
FINISHED PLACE MAT: 13½″ × 23″
FINISHED TABLE RUNNER: 13½″ × 61″
FINISHED COASTER: 7″ per side

This coordinated set consists of a matched set of four generously sized place mats, a long table runner, and six large triangular coasters. It is a bit different from the other projects in the book, as the instructions here are to make the full matching set all at once. By making the whole set, you get to efficiently use up (and, of course, show off!) a whole collection of your favorite seasonal fabrics.

MATERIALS

These materials are enough to make the complete dining set. Yardages are based on fabric at least 40″ wide.

White fabric: ⅔ yard for ghost blocks

Black fabric: ⅛ yard for ghost blocks

Assorted Halloween fabrics (11): ¼ yard each for plain blocks

Marking pen

Binding: ⅞ yard

Backing: 2¾ yards

Batting:
• 4 pieces 17 x 27
• 1 piece 17″ × 65″
• Several small scraps for coasters

Perle cotton: Black or gray for accent quilting

CUTTING

White and black fabrics for ghost blocks

• Referring to Basic Triangular Ghost Block (page 43), follow the cutting and sewing instructions to make 9 blocks.

NOTE The fastest and most efficient way to cut everything is to cut all 9 of each individual piece at once. Cut strips across the width of fabric and then subcut those pieces.

Assorted Halloween fabrics for blocks

From *each* fabric:

• Cut 1 strip 7″ × width of fabric.

Using the 60° triangle ruler, subcut 7 of the 60° triangles, using the 7″ measurement. This will give you 77 triangles. You will use 67 to make the place mats, table runner, and coasters. The extra 10 are for design decisions and mistakes. And then, of those, use 6 for the back of the coasters. So really you will use all but 4 triangles by the end.

Binding

• Cut 12 strips 2¼″ × width of fabric.

Batting scraps

• Cut 6 triangles 60°, each 7″ in length.

Boo's Coming to Dinner? Place Mats *and* Table Runner

You can design the place mats and table runner together!

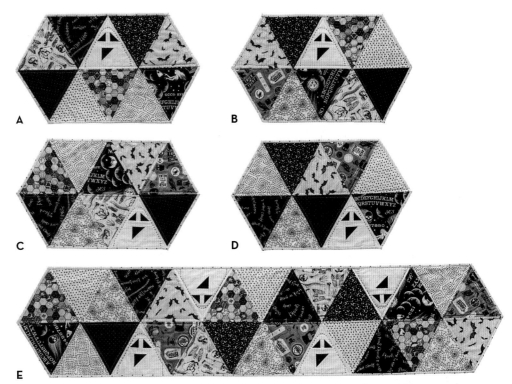

Use a ¼″ seam allowance and press the seams open.

1. Refer to Basic Triangular Ghost Block (page 43) to make 9 ghost block triangles. You will use 8 triangles for the place mats and table runner. (Set the last triangle aside for the coasters; see Boo's Coming to Dinner? Coasters, page 46.)

2. Arrange the triangles following the place mat assembly diagrams A and B (below). For each place mat, you will need 9 Halloween fabric triangles and 1 ghost block triangle. Note the position of the ghost block. Make 2 place mats according to diagram A and 2 place mats according to diagram B. When positioned around the table, the ghosts will be right side up for each person at each place.

> **tip** Mix and match the various fabrics throughout all the pieces of the dining set. It may help you to sort all the fabrics first into little piles of what will be used for which pieces. Or design all the pieces at once by arranging everything on a design wall.

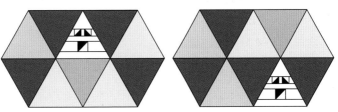

Place mat assembly A and B

3. Arrange the triangles following the table runner assembly diagram. Use 26 Halloween fabric triangles and 4 ghost block triangles.

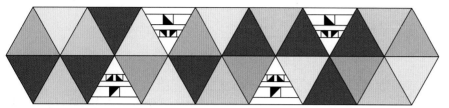
Table runner assembly

4. For each place mat and the table runner, sew the triangles in each row together. Press. Sew the rows together. Press.

Place on the table. Try not to spill on them ...
(or at least not before you show them to a quilting friend).

Boo's Coming to Dinner? Coasters

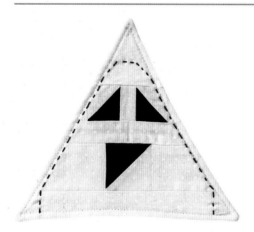

1. Use 5 Halloween fabric triangles and 1 ghost block triangle to make the coaster fronts. For the backs, choose 6 of the leftover Halloween triangles.

2. For each coaster, place the front and back pieces right sides together, and then place a batting triangle on top.

3. Sew around the outside through all 3 layers with a slightly larger than ¼" seam. Leave a 1½" opening on the bottom edge for turning.

4. Trim the seam allowance at the corners and turn inside out. Be sure the corners are really poked all the way out.

FINISH THE PLACE MATS AND TABLE RUNNER

Machine quilt as desired. Then, using the perle cotton, hand stitch to gently round out the appearance of the ghost shapes, as if they are hiding against the white blocks. Bind.

5. Press. Be sure the fabric at the opening is nicely folded inside. Topstitch ⅛"–¼" from the edge all the way around the outside of the coaster. This will catch and close the opening, and it's also a decorative element.

6. Add hand quilting, using perle cotton on the ghost coaster.

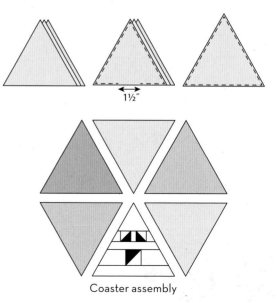
Coaster assembly

When not in use, arrange your coasters in a hexagon shape on your table. Cool, right?

about the author

RIEL NASON is an award-winning novelist and quilter. She is best known for her whimsical selvage quilts and bold use of color. Her favorite holiday of the year (by far!) is Halloween, and since 2010 she has made more than 60 unique Halloween quilts and sewn projects. Her debut solo quilting exhibition was a series of selvage quilts that incorporated Halloween, humor, and quilting. It was called *A ¼-Inch Scream*. Riel lives in New Brunswick, Canada, with her family. Visit her website at rielnason.com.

Also by Riel Nason:

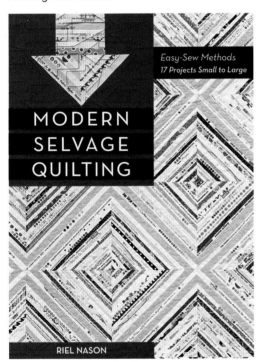

Photo by Shane Nason

Want even more creative content?

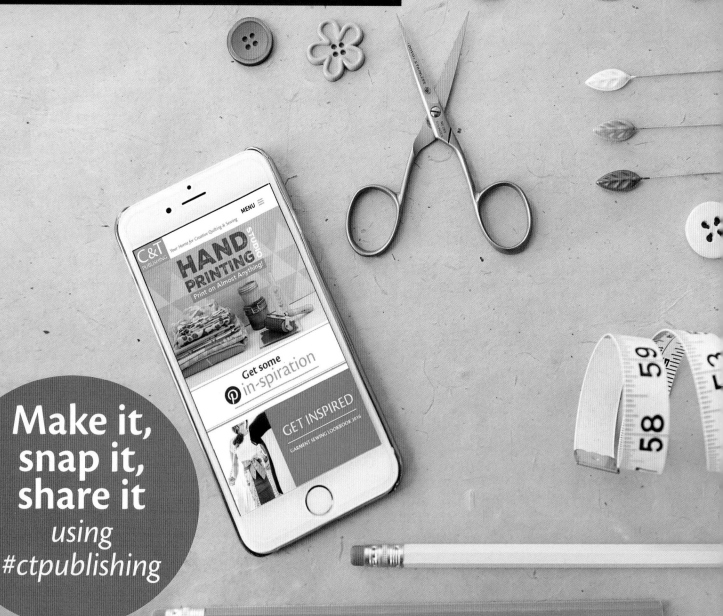

Make it, snap it, share it *using #ctpublishing*